Wind Power

by Stephanie Fitzgerald

**Science and Curriculum Consultant:
Debra Voege, M.A.,
Science Curriculum Resource Teacher**

CHELSEA CLUBHOUSE
An Imprint of Chelsea House Publishers

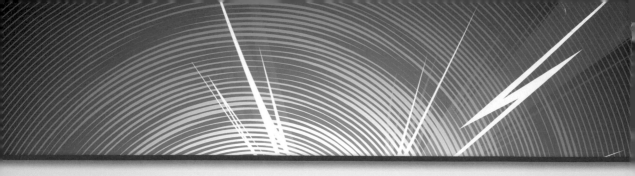

Energy Today: Wind Power

Copyright © 2010 by Infobase Publishing

Chelsea Clubhouse
An imprint of Chelsea House Publishers
132 West 31st Street
New York NY 10001

Library of Congress Cataloging-in-Publication Data
Fitzgerald, Stephanie.
      Wind power / by Stephanie Fitzgerald; science and curriculum consultant, Debra Voege.
          p. cm. — (Energy today)
      Includes index.
      ISBN 978-1-60413-780-4
      1. Wind power--Juvenile literature. I. Title. II. Series.
   TJ820.F572 2010
   333.9'2—dc22   2009038924

Chelsea Clubhouse books are available at special discounts when purchased in bulk quantities for businesses, associations, institutions, or sales promotions. Please call our Special Sales Department in New York at (212) 967-8800 or (800) 322-8755.

You can find Chelsea Clubhouse on the World Wide Web at http://www.chelseahouse.com

Developed for Chelsea House by RJF Publishing LLC (www.RJFpublishing.com)
Project Editor: Jacqueline Laks Gorman
Text and cover design by Tammy West/Westgraphix LLC
Illustrations by Spectrum Creative Inc.
Photo research by Edward A. Thomas
Index by Nila Glikin
Composition by Westgraphix LLC
Cover printed by Bang Printing, Brainerd, MN
Book printed and bound by Bang Printing, Brainerd, MN
Date printed: May 2010
Printed in the United States of America

Photo Credits: 5: (top) iStockphoto, (bottom) Africa Windmill Project; 7: iStockphoto; 8: AP Images; 16: iStockphoto; 17: iStockphoto; 19: From the collection of Carl Wilcox; 21: iStockphoto; 25: iStockphoto; 26: © BETTMANN/CORBIS; 27: iStockphoto; 30: © Paul Glendell/Alamy; 33: Ole Christiansen/EON; 34: iStockphoto; 36: James Hager/Robert Harding Travel/Photolibrary; 37: © Nick Hanna/Alamy; 39: Ben Shepard/Sky WindPower; 40: AP Images; 41: Magenn Power Inc.; 42: Courtesy of Dr. Maria Skyllas-Kazacos.

10 9 8 7 6 5 4 3 2 1

This book is printed on acid-free paper.

All links and Web addresses were checked and verified to be correct at the time of publication. Because of the dynamic nature of the Web, some addresses and links may have changed since publication and may no longer be valid.

TABLE OF CONTENTS

CHAPTER 1:
Energy from the Wind 4

CHAPTER 2:
How Does Wind Energy Work? 14

CHAPTER 3:
The Advantages of Wind Energy 24

CHAPTER 4:
Possible Problems with Wind Energy 32

CHAPTER 5:
What Is the Future of Wind Energy? 38

Glossary 44

To Learn More 46

Index 47

Words that are defined in the Glossary are in **bold** type the first time they appear in the text.

Energy from the Wind

Energy is an essential part of life. We use energy to move and to breathe. We even use it when we are sleeping! This energy is supplied by the food we eat. We also use energy to power the things that make our lives easier and more comfortable. We use fuel in vehicles and to heat our homes. We use electricity to run lights, computers, and televisions. This energy has mainly been supplied by **fossil fuels**, such as coal, oil, and natural gas. More and more, however, people are looking to new sources of energy—such as wind—to power our world.

Put simply, wind is moving air. This type of energy—the energy of motion—is called **kinetic** energy. Although we cannot see the air moving, we can feel it. The wind might be a soft breeze that barely ruffles our hair or a strong gust that pushes us from one spot to another. Throughout history, people have captured the energy from moving air and used it to power vehicles, such as sailboats, or to operate machinery, such as windmills.

Early Windmills

The windmill was the first machine designed to use the power of wind to do work. Early windmills were invented in the Middle East. They were used to pump water and to grind grain into flour. These windmills looked very different from the

traditional Dutch windmills most people picture when they think of these machines. The first windmills used up to 12 sails, which hung from **horizontal** poles attached to a **vertical** post. (A horizontal pole runs parallel to the ground; a vertical post is up and down, at a right angle to the ground.) In the case of a grinding mill, the grinding stone was attached to the same vertical post. The wind would cause the post to rotate, or turn, which caused the grinding stone to move. This is called a **panemone** design. Because the sails hang down all around the post, this type of windmill can catch the wind from any direction. The sails of these windmills do not have to be turned into the wind.

Windmills were introduced in Europe in the twelfth century. According to some historians, soldiers returning from the Crusades carried the idea for the structures home with them from the Middle

Panemone windmills were invented hundreds of years ago. Shown here: a current project to build such windmills in African villages.

Did You Know?

The First Windmills

It is believed that the earliest known windmill was invented in Persia (today, Afghanistan and Iran), around 500 to 900 A.D. There are no drawings of this windmill, however, only written descriptions. The first documented windmill design—which we do have pictures of—is also from the Middle East. It featured vertical sails that were made of bundles of reeds or wood. These types of windmills were also used in China, possibly as early as more than 2,000 years ago. The first documented evidence of a windmill in China, however, was not until 1219 A.D.

East. (During the Crusades, which occurred during medieval times, Christians from Europe fought to take control of the Holy Land from Muslims.) The first illustrations of a European windmill are from 1270 A.D. They show a design that is different from the Middle Eastern type of windmill. The European windmill featured four sails, or blades, mounted on a horizontal post, which was attached to a gear inside the building. A vertical post inside the building was attached to the same gear. As the horizontal post spun, it moved the gear, which turned the vertical post. The vertical post provided power to a grinding stone. This type of windmill was called a post mill. The entire structure could be **manually** rotated so that the blades would be facing into the wind.

The structure was later improved so that only the top of the mill, where the blades were mounted, moved—not the entire structure. This type of windmill was called a tower mill. In the eighteenth century,

Traditional windmills used the power of the wind to grind grain or pump water.

another improvement came in the form of something called a fantail. This small wheel, mounted at the top of the tower mill, automatically turns the blades into the wind.

Generating Electricity

People around the world still use windmills for the traditional tasks of raising water or grinding grain. Since the early 1980s, however, people have been using wind power to generate electricity. There is a great deal of excitement about using wind power to generate electricity because the wind is a completely **renewable**, clean source of energy. The same cannot be said for the fossil fuels that supply the majority of energy in the world today.

To create electricity, most **power plants**, or power stations, burn fossil fuels to boil water. The steam produced by the boiling water is then heated further so that it has enough pressure to turn the blades on devices called **turbines**. The blades are on one end of a long pole, or rod. The rod is connected to a **generator**. The generator uses large magnets and metal coils to produce electricity.

Here is what happens. As the turbines spin, they make the rods turn. When the rods turn, either a magnet or a coil turns inside the generator. This causes an electric current to flow. The current then makes its way along transmission lines to homes, schools, office buildings, and wherever it is needed. Today, power plants are linked through a system—which is known as the **grid**—to carry electricity through transmission lines across large distances.

Did You Know?
The Power of Wind

The wind can blow at incredible speeds and can be very destructive. In May 1999, wind speeds inside a tornado in Oklahoma reached an amazing 318 miles (512 kilometers) per hour. That is the fastest wind speed ever recorded. The tornado killed 40 people and destroyed thousands of homes. The record for wind speed that is not associated with a tornado was set on April 12, 1934, on Mount Washington in New Hampshire. That day, a gust of wind measured 231 miles (372 kilometers) per hour.

The destruction caused by the 1999 tornado in Oklahoma.

What Are Fossil Fuels?

As plants and animals die, they **decompose** (break down) in the earth. Over time, they become covered with layers of dirt. After millions of years, these plant and animal remains turn into fossil fuels. Fossil fuels can be solid, liquid, or gaseous—coal, oil, or natural gas. People burn fossil fuels to produce energy. A home, for example, may be heated by oil or natural gas. A power plant may burn coal to produce electricity. For many years, fossil fuels have been a readily available, fairly inexpensive way to provide energy, so they have been widely used. In fact, fossil fuels currently provide 85 percent of the energy used in the United States. Unfortunately, however, there are problems associated with people's dependence on fossil fuels.

Fossil fuels are called **nonrenewable** energy sources. It took millions of years for the fossil fuels we rely on today to form. Once we have used up all of the coal, oil, and natural gas currently under Earth's surface, there will be no more coal, oil, or natural gas to replace them. Fossil fuels are being used much faster than they can form. It is impossible to determine exactly how much longer these resources will last. Many experts think, however, that our coal reserves may not last longer than 130 more years. They expect oil and natural gas to run out even sooner.

Fossil Fuels and the Environment

Another problem with fossil fuels is the negative impact they have on the **environment**. Burning fossil fuels creates a type of pollution called soot. These tiny particles mix with water particles in the sky to create **smog**—a gray-brown haze that hangs in the air. Smog has been linked to lung disorders such

9

Did You Know?

London's Fatal Fog

During the winter of 1952, London, England, experienced an unusually cold spell. People burned more coal than usual in an attempt to keep warm. As a result, thousands of tons of black soot and sulfur dioxide were released into the air. During the week of December 5, an estimated 12,000 Londoners were killed by the "fatal fog" created by the coal fires. At its peak, on December 8 and 9, the death toll reached 900 people per day! As a result of this tragedy, the British government passed its first Clean Air Act in 1956. The law allowed local governments to provide money to homeowners to convert their coal-burning stoves to use cleaner sources of energy.

as bronchitis and asthma. According to experts, the pollution from coal-fired plants is responsible for more than 23,000 premature (early) deaths in the United States every year. In contrast, the technology used in the wind industry gives off no harmful **emissions**. The wind industry has recorded only one death among members of the public (people who are not wind industry workers) in 20 years of operation. The person killed was a German skydiver who flew off course and parachuted into a wind plant.

When coal and oil are burned, they give off, or emit, sulfur dioxide and nitrogen oxides. When these chemicals mix with other compounds in the **atmosphere**, such as water and oxygen, they create a toxic (poisonous) solution of sulfuric acid and nitric acid. If these chemicals are present in areas where there is wet weather, they create **acid rain** (which also includes acid fog, snow, and mist). Acid rain can harm and even kill trees, fish, and other living creatures where it falls. In the United States, about two-thirds of all sulfur dioxide and one-quarter of nitrogen oxides in the air come from power plants that create electricity by burning fossil fuels such as coal.

The burning of fossil fuels also releases **greenhouse gases**, such as **carbon dioxide** and methane. Some greenhouses gases are found naturally in Earth's atmosphere. They help keep the planet's temperature stable. Sunlight passes through the atmosphere to strike Earth. Some of the **solar** energy is absorbed, and a large amount of it bounces back toward space. Some of the solar energy that bounces back is trapped by the greenhouse gases that are naturally in the atmosphere. If the right amount of solar energy is radiated back into space, the surface temperature of Earth will remain generally constant. Unfortunately, the emission of greenhouse gases—such as those created by burning fossil fuels—is upsetting this balance.

In the past 150 years, there has been a 25 percent increase in the level of certain greenhouse gases, especially carbon dioxide, in the atmosphere. Normally, the process of plant **photosynthesis** naturally regulates concentrations of carbon

In Their Own Words

"[W]ind power can provide 20 percent of the nation's electricity by 2030, and be a critical part of the solution to global warming. This level of wind power is the equivalent of taking 140 million cars off the road."

Randall Swisher, former executive director, American Wind Energy Association dioxide. Unfortunately, human activity produces so many tons of carbon dioxide emissions that there is too much for the world's plant life to absorb. This imbalance has led to an ongoing increase in concentrations of greenhouse gases in the atmosphere. Experts have determined that, over time, the rising concentration of these gases will produce an increase in Earth's surface temperature. Most scientists believe that these rising temperatures may lead to changes in sea level, precipitation (such as rainfall), and the seriousness of storms. This warming of Earth's surface and atmosphere is commonly referred to as **global warming** or global **climate** change.

Climate change could affect every part of the planet. As **glaciers** and large sheets of ice start to melt, sea levels could rise, causing small islands and coastal lands to become flooded. As the glaciers continue to shrink, other areas that rely on glacial run-off from mountains for fresh water could face a severe shortage of water. Rainfall in other areas could decrease drastically.

A Sustainable Solution

Global demand for all forms of energy is expected to grow by more than 44 percent by the year 2030. Since there are problems associated with the traditional use of fossil fuels, many people think that finding alternative energy sources—**sustainable** energy sources—should be a priority. Sustainable energy sources can help meet the world's needs without harming the environment or depleting all of the resources. To meet that goal, experts are looking at renewable energy sources, such as wind, solar, and water power.

Wind energy is one of the fastest growing energy fields in the world. The global capacity for wind power (in other words,

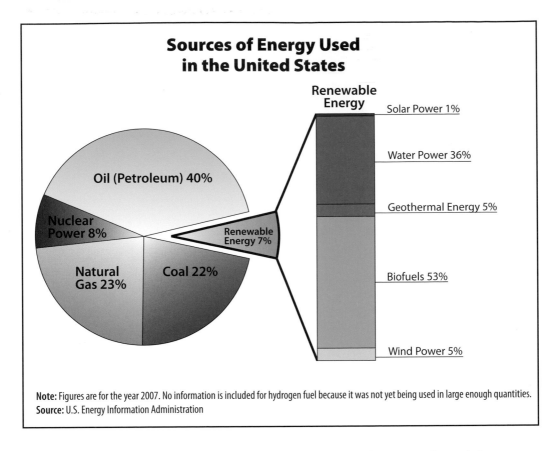

Sources of Energy Used in the United States

Oil (Petroleum) 40%

Nuclear Power 8%

Natural Gas 23%

Coal 22%

Renewable Energy 7%

Renewable Energy

Solar Power 1%

Water Power 36%

Geothermal Energy 5%

Biofuels 53%

Wind Power 5%

Note: Figures are for the year 2007. No information is included for hydrogen fuel because it was not yet being used in large enough quantities.
Source: U.S. Energy Information Administration

the ability to produce electricity and other forms of usable energy from wind power) increased 27 percent in 2007. In 2008, the United States added 8,358 **megawatts** (MW) of wind-powered electricity. That is enough to power 2 million homes. Currently, wind power supplies only 5 percent of the energy used in the United States. The U.S. Department of Energy (DOE) wants that to increase to 20 percent by 2030.

Right now, wind power is used to supplement (add to) other forms of electricity. It cannot meet all of the energy needs of the United States now—or even in the near future. There are several factors that limit our ability to rely more strongly on the wind for electricity. However, improvements in technology continue to propel wind power in the right direction.

CHAPTER 2

How Does Wind Energy Work?

We will never run out of wind, which makes it a great source of renewable energy. When the Sun heats Earth's atmosphere, it creates warm air. As the warm air spreads out and rises, it is replaced by colder, denser air. We call this movement of the air *wind*. For thousands of years, farmers have used the power of the wind to pump water or grind grain. Today, people are capturing the wind's energy and turning it into electricity. The modern windmills they use are called wind turbines. Farmers, homeowners, and even some businesses may use wind turbines to generate a portion of their electricity. They rely on back-up generators to supply power when the wind is not blowing.

Most attention today is focused on larger scale projects, however, such as commercial wind farms. Power plants can use wind turbines—rather than steam—to generate electricity. Used on a large scale, wind power can have a significant effect on the growing global need for more energy and efforts to stop climate change.

Wind Turbines

A wind turbine consists of a pole or tower, blades, and a special box called a **nacelle**. Each turbine can produce electricity. Wind turbines come in a variety of shapes and sizes, but the two basic designs are the *horizontal axis* and the *vertical axis*.

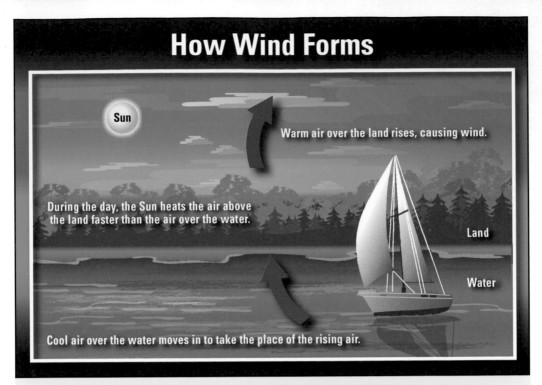

How Wind Forms

Sun

Warm air over the land rises, causing wind.

During the day, the Sun heats the air above the land faster than the air over the water.

Land

Water

Cool air over the water moves in to take the place of the rising air.

Wind develops because the air above water and land absorb heat from the Sun at different rates. The warm air rises, and the cool air moves in to take its place.

The horizontal axis design is the more common of the two. Here, two or three rotor blades are attached to the tower by a shaft that runs parallel to the ground. The blades have to be turned to face the wind. The turbine is designed to do this automatically. In the vertical axis design, the main shaft and blades are upright, at a right angle to the ground. The blades do not have to be rotated. With this type of design, the blades are able to catch the wind from whatever direction it is blowing.

Regardless of design, the rotor has to be mounted to a tower. The farther you get from the ground, the stronger the wind blows. This results in more energy produced, so taller towers are most efficient. The towers for large commercial turbines can be more than 300 feet (91 meters) tall. They can have blades that are between 165 feet (50 meters) and 295 feet (90 meters) long.

The tall tower and blades of a modern wind turbine. This turbine has a horizontal axis design.

There is more to a turbine's efficiency than height, however. Having enough wind is important, but there is actually a fine line between enough wind speed and too much. A typical turbine requires wind speeds of about 9 miles (14.5 kilometers) per hour to start. This is referred to as the *cut-in speed*. However, wind speeds of 55 miles (88.5 kilometers) per hour or more will actually damage the turbine. The forces produced by the rapidly spinning blades could rip them completely from the rotor. To protect against this problem, the larger turbines have automatic systems that measure wind speed and direction and adjust the blades accordingly. If the blades are spinning too quickly, they may be tilted so that they are not catching all of the wind. The turbines also have brakes that can slow and even stop the blades as necessary. Most turbines produce electricity using an average wind speed of about 13 miles (21 kilometers) per hour.

In addition to the tower and blades, the other visible part of the horizontal-axis turbine is the nacelle, which is the box directly behind the blades. That is where the kinetic energy of the wind is turned into electricity. In most turbines, the blades are attached to an **axle**, or shaft, that runs into the nacelle and is attached to a gearbox. The gearbox has an important job. The job of the gearbox is to increase the speed of the axle's rotation from about 50 revolutions per minute (rpm) to 1,800 rpm.

Did You Know?

A Cleaner Solution

A large commercial wind turbine can produce enough electricity to power as many as 300 homes per year. Using fossil fuels to provide the same amount of energy would result in the emission of about 2,800 tons (2,540 metric tons) of carbon dioxide.

Wind turbines at Altamont Pass, California, one of the largest wind farms in the world.

Did You Know?

Watts and More

The amount of electricity produced is measured in **watts**. A kilowatt (kW) equals 1,000 watts, a megawatt (MW) equals one million watts, a gigawatt (GW) equals one billion watts, and a terawatt (tW) equals one trillion watts. Electricity is usually measured in kilowatt-hours (kWh)—or one kilowatt consumed for one hour. For example, if you leave a 50-watt light bulb on for 20 hours, it will use up 1 kWh of electricity (50 watts x 20 hours = 1,000 watt hours or 1 kWh). The average U.S. household consumes about 10,000 kWh of electricity per year. A 10-kW wind turbine can generate enough power for a typical household. A 5-MW turbine can power more than 1,400 households.

The axle that is attached to the blades is called a low-speed shaft. There is also an axle, called the high-speed shaft, that comes out of the gearbox. The high-speed shaft spins inside a generator, where it produces electricity. The electricity is then sent along cables to the power grid, where it is combined with electricity from other sources and sent to customers.

The most common application for wind power is commercial. Individual homeowners, however, can also use this technology to generate electricity for their house. Small residential turbines— also known as micro wind turbines—can be installed on top of a house and "plugged in" the existing electrical system. In this case, the house gets its electricity from both the turbine and the local utility company. When wind speeds are too low for the turbine to spin, electricity is provided

PALMER PUTNAM

Palmer Putnam was born in 1900. He graduated from the Massachusetts Institute of Technology in 1923 and became an engineer. Putnam had a house in Cape Cod, Massachusetts, where it was very windy. Electricity for the house cost a great deal of money. Putnam thought that wind might be used to generate electricity for less money. In 1941, to see if his idea could work, he built the world's first really large wind turbine (shown in the photo here). The turbine, which was 110 feet (33 meters) tall, sat on top of a mountain in Vermont called Grandpa's Knob and generated 1.25 megawatts (MW) of electricity. The turbine failed in March 1945, when strong winds tore off one of its blades. Before becoming interested in wind energy, Putnam had worked as a geologist in Africa, flew planes for the British during World War I, and spent time as president of his family's New York publishing company, G.P. Putnam's Sons. During World War II, he did research for the U.S. government. Afterward, he wrote a number of books about different sources of energy, including nuclear energy. Putnam died in 1984.

the traditional way—from the utility company. When the wind increases, so does the power generated by the turbine. The utility company then contributes less power.

Altamont Pass, California

Altamont Pass in California is a wind farm that is located in a valley, just one hour's drive from San Francisco. The San Francisco Bay area and Pacific Ocean lie on one side of the site. The San Joaquin Valley lies on the other. This location is particularly good for a wind farm because the hot air from the valley pulls in the cooler air from the ocean, creating winds that blow steadily across Altamont Pass. The site, which is one of the world's first wind farms, is also the largest concentration of wind turbines in the world. It contains more than 5,000 turbines that produce 1.1 terawatt-hours (tWh) of electricity per year.

Wind Farms

Utility companies need to provide power to many households, so they rely on groups of turbines to generate electricity. These turbines are clustered together on large tracts of land called wind farms. The power generated by each turbine on the wind farm is added together.

In addition to all of the individual wind turbines, a large-scale wind farm that would serve a utility company includes an underground power transmission system, maintenance facilities, and a substation that connects the farm to the company's power grid. The best places for wind farms have fast, steady winds. Open plains are good because there are few trees or buildings to block the wind. Together, such states as North Dakota, Kansas, and Texas, which have a great deal of open land, are actually windy enough to power the entire United States! Coastal areas are good for the same reason. Valleys, where wind is funneled between mountains, are also prime spots for building wind farms.

The wind turbines also have to be located in the right place on the farm. Engineers want to place the towers close together so the maximum number of turbines can be fit into a limited space. They have to make certain, however, that the turbines don't "shade" each other, or block each other's wind. The best space between turbines seems to be between five to seven times the diameter of the rotor.

Off the Shore

Wind farms can also be located offshore, in the water, where winds tend to blow stronger and more steadily—and turbines can be built even bigger. These sites are also appealing because they tend to be close to big population areas. It is easier to run electricity from the Atlantic Ocean to New York City,

Vertical axis wind turbines, such as the ones shown here, are not as common as turbines with a horizontal axis design.

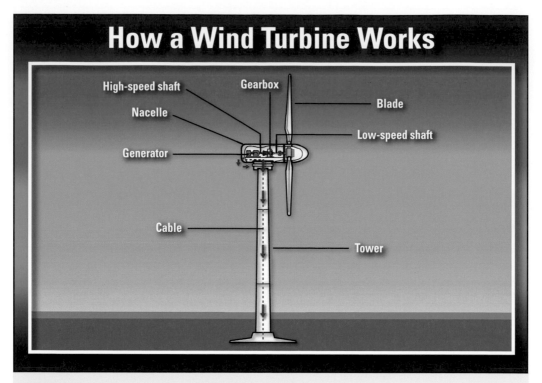

How a Wind Turbine Works

High-speed shaft

Gearbox

Nacelle

Blade

Generator

Low-speed shaft

Cable

Tower

Wind makes the blades of the turbine turn. The blades spin the shafts inside the nacelle and gearbox. The high-speed shaft spins the generator, which produces electricity that is sent along cables to the power grid.

for example, than to run it from North Dakota to New York. (Underwater cables are used to carry the electricity to shore.) Offshore projects are currently more popular in Europe—where the countries are more densely populated—than in the United States. Developers are looking carefully at possible offshore sites in the United States, however. In fact, a major wind farm, which would be called Cape Wind, has been proposed for Nantucket Sound south of Cape Cod, Massachusetts.

Currently, offshore wind farms are being built only in shallow water close to the shore. The supports that are used to anchor turbines to the sea floor can be used only in water that is less than about 100 feet (30 meters) deep. This is not ideal, because stronger winds are usually found farther out to sea. (Engineers hope to solve this problem in the future by building floating platforms for the turbines.) Since the turbines are located fairly close to land, they can be visible from the shore, and some people do not like this. For example, some people who are opposed to the Cape Wind project object to the fact that the turbines will be visible.

Construction of the world's largest offshore wind farm is set to begin in 2011 off the southeast coast of England in the Thames Estuary. (An estuary is a place where freshwater rivers and streams flow into the sea.) Three international companies are involved in the 90-square-mile (233-square-kilometer) project, which is called the London Array. In the first phase of the project, 175 turbines will start producing 630 MW of electricity by the year 2012. The ultimate goal for the Array is 341 turbines producing 1,000 MW of electricity. That is enough to power hundreds of thousands of homes, or one-fourth of all the homes in Greater London.

In Their Own Words

"The United States has some of the best wind resources in the world ...North and South Dakota, theoretically, have enough wind to power the whole country. The challenge is tapping that and transmission and distribution. But if you look at the center of the country, the wind resources are tremendous. If you look at the coastlines, the...resources are tremendous."

Vic Abate, vice president of Renewables, GE Energy

CHAPTER 3

The Advantages of Wind Energy

As more wind farms are built, the United States is beginning to get closer to the goal set by the Department of Energy of obtaining 20 percent of the country's energy supply from wind by the year 2030. It is clear that the benefits of wind power will touch many areas of life.

One obvious benefit is the environmental impact of not relying as much on fossil fuels. If wind power produced 20 percent of U.S. electricity by the year 2030, carbon dioxide emissions would be cut by 25 percent. The reduction in emissions of gases linked to global warming would be equal to removing 71 million cars from the roads or planting 104 million acres (42 million hectares) of trees. There would also be an impact on water. Generating electricity using fossil fuels takes a great deal of water, while making electricity with wind power does not. An increase in wind-powered electricity would decrease the amount of water required for the production of electricity by 4 trillion gallons (15 trillion liters).

Cleaning up the environment is not the only benefit to choosing alternative energy sources such as wind power. Coal, oil, and natural gas are being used up. New sources of energy must be found. Together with other renewable sources, such as solar energy, wind power can help provide energy for the future.

Burning coal causes a great deal of pollution, including smog. Coal emissions have also been linked to global warming.

Less Foreign Oil

Increasing the amount of power from wind energy would also lead to less use of foreign oil, which has important political effects. Right now, the United States—and much of the world—relies on just a few countries for its supply of fossil fuels, especially oil. Some of those countries are Saudi Arabia, Iran, Kuwait, and Iraq. This gives these Middle Eastern countries a great deal of power in world politics.

In 1960, the Organization of Petroleum Exporting Countries (OPEC) was formed by some of the world's main producers of oil. In 1973, members of OPEC worked together to raise oil prices. They also placed an **embargo** on shipments of oil to the United States and a number of other nations. (They were protesting support for Israel on the part of the United States and the other nations during a war Israel was fighting with Egypt and Syria.) The price of gas jumped, and there was a

Did You Know?

No Gas!

In 1973, during the oil embargo, OPEC raised the price of oil in addition to decreasing the supply. As a result, the price of oil went from $3 a barrel to $12. Ordinary Americans felt the strain at the gas pump, where restrictions were put in place. U.S. drivers whose vehicle license plates ended in an odd number could purchase gas only on odd-numbered days of the month. Drivers whose license plates ended in even numbers could buy gas only on even-numbered days of the month. In some areas, stations used a three-flag system to indicate the availability of gas. If a green flag was flying, anyone could buy gas. A yellow flag meant there were restrictions on the sale of gas. A red flag meant the station had no gas for sale. In the last week of February 1974, 20 percent of U.S. gas stations had no fuel at all.

Drivers lined up for gas during the 1973 oil embargo.

serious energy crisis with fuel shortages in the United States and Canada. The oil embargo led many U.S. government leaders to think about and support the development of alternative energy.

A Different Kind of Green

There are also important economic reasons to embrace wind technology. Wind power can provide income for U.S. farmers by letting them **lease** land to wind farm developers. (Most wind developers are private companies that then sell the electricity to power companies.) The small towns that lease land to developers will also benefit. There will be jobs for people who build and maintain

Cows and other livestock graze right at the base of wind turbines.

Did You Know?

Careers in Wind

Someone who likes to work with his or her hands—and is not afraid of heights—would be well suited to a job as a wind technician. There are countless other job opportunities in the field, too. For example, energy analysts conduct studies to determine if a project will be profitable, as well as how it will impact a community. Engineers plan and design turbines and wind farms, and attorneys work on preparing legislation (measures that need to be passed by the government) and drawing up lease agreements. There are also plenty of jobs for people who do not specifically have "energy" experience. The jobs available at energy companies are just like jobs found in other offices, from receptionists and graphic designers to bookkeepers and human resources managers.

the turbines. Also, local businesses will have more customers as people from the development company come to town to work on the project.

Most wind farms in the United States are located on land that is already being used for agriculture. Although maintenance roads leading to the turbines are needed, the rest of the land surrounding the structures is not disturbed. Livestock can—and do—graze right up to the base of the turbines, and crops can grow next to them.

Typically, a farmer leases his or her land to a commercial wind developer. The developer owns, builds, installs, and maintains the turbines. The farmer does not own any of the equipment and is not responsible for any of it. The developer pays the farmer a fee for use of the land. If wind capacity in the United States is increased to 20 percent by the year 2030, the increase in revenue for local communities could be more than $1.5 billion per year.

Creating New Jobs

This rapidly developing industry will also create thousands of new jobs. In order to meet the DOE's wind power goal for 2030, the manufacturing, construction, and installation of wind turbines and related equipment will have to be increased. In addition, although the turbines run without any human action, wind technicians are always needed to perform maintenance and any repairs—up to and including changing a light bulb at the top of a 300-foot (91-meter) tower! All of this will translate into 150,000 brand new jobs. Perhaps 500,000 more jobs will be created in related fields—those that support the wind industry but are not directly part of it—such as trucking and shipping.

Increasing the Availability

There was a time when electricity from wind-powered sources cost more than from traditional sources. That is no longer true. In 1981, electricity from wind cost about 25¢ per kilowatt-hour. This has dropped to between 4¢ and 6¢ per kilowatt-

In Their Own Words

"It's just another crop that we harvest. It's much easier than harvesting our other crops....As long as the turbine is turning, we know we're [going to] get paid."

Donna Griffin, farm owner, Fenner, New York

In Their Own Words

"If you have a certain set of skills, you can work for anybody. But if you happen to believe that we as a society need to have clean, renewable energy that doesn't use fuel or water, the wind industry is a prime fit. There's plenty of room for folks who...want to help society not ruin itself by continuing to burn coal."

Michael Wiener, American Wind Energy Association

hour in recent years. This is similar to the average rate paid by consumers for electricity from coal-fired plants. According to the DOE, the price for wind-powered electricity should continue to fall as technology improves. Nevertheless, not

A worker on the job on top of a turbine. Anyone doing such work cannot be afraid of heights.

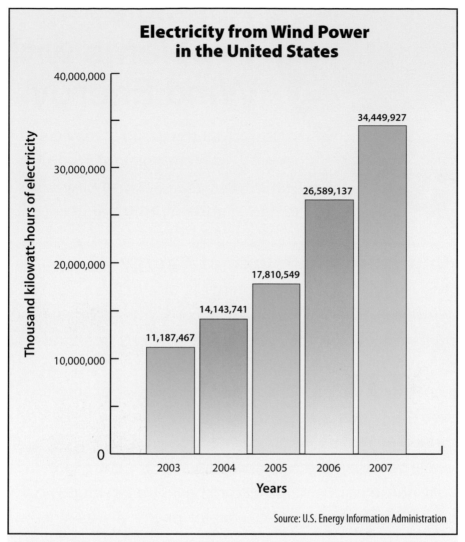

Electricity from Wind Power in the United States

Thousand kilowatt-hours of electricity

40,000,000	
30,000,000	
20,000,000	
10,000,000	
0	

11,187,467

14,143,741

17,810,549

26,589,137

34,449,927

2003   2004   2005   2006   2007

Years

Source: U.S. Energy Information Administration

The amount of electricity generated by wind power has increased steadily in recent years.

many people currently have access to this type of electricity. Wind power is a fast-growing technology, but it is still relatively new. There are a number of different problems that will need to be resolved before wind-powered electricity can be made more readily available to a greater number of people in the United States and the rest of the world.

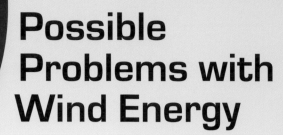

CHAPTER 4

Possible Problems with Wind Energy

Despite all the positive aspects of wind energy, some people are not in favor of it. Arguments against wind power include both economic and environmental complaints.

An Unpredictable Source of Energy

One key problem with wind energy is that it is unpredictable. The wind is renewable, but it is not constant. Turbines produce electricity only when they are spinning. If it is not windy, no electricity is produced, even if people need it. This problem does not affect traditional coal-fired plants, for example, because the plants always have fossil fuels ready to be burned to produce electricity when it is needed.

People who depend on wind power to generate electricity for their home or business need to have a back-up power source. The problem is not critical for power plants since wind-generated electricity generally makes up only a portion of the overall power they provide to their customers.

There are also different problems with transmission. Many of the best sites for wind farms—such as on the open plains of the Midwest—are located far from the more densely populated urban areas that consume the most energy. Can large amounts of electricity be transported over long distances, so that the large numbers of energy users can get the power they need? Developers need to either tie into existing lines or install new high-voltage wires. Installing new wires will likely cost thousands of dollars per mile.

Too Pricey?

Some people also complain that wind turbines are expensive to build and install. It is expensive to build a wind farm. Construction of the London Array, for example, will cost almost $5 billion per GW. The London Array is an offshore site, and the cost of building such a facility is more expensive than building a land-based site because the towers have to be bigger and stronger to withstand waves and the **corrosive** effects of salt water. Offshore sites also require longer transmission lines. Of course, the construction also has to take place on—and under—the water!

The typical cost of a large-scale wind farm built on land

The Rodsand Wind Park, an offshore wind farm in Denmark.

is about $2.5 billion. A typical coal-fired power station can cost around $2 billion to build. A nuclear-powered station can cost between $2 billion and $3 billion. (The range in cost has to do with the size of the plant and how much energy it produces.)

Supporters of wind power argue that these numbers do not reflect the true cost of the different systems. They claim that in calculating the cost of an energy source, we should include something called external—or social—costs. These are the effects that using a particular energy source has on the environment and human health, among other things. Though these costs can be hard to calculate, a 10-year study conducted by the European Union suggests that the real cost of producing electricity is cheaper with wind power than with coal. That is because wind power has very few external costs. It does not have any associated health risks (such as the lung disease linked to soot and smog), and it does not hurt the environment.

Environmental Menace?

Some critics of wind power are not concerned about the effectiveness of wind technology. They are more concerned about the turbines themselves. Some people who live near wind farms have complained that the large turbines are ruining the natural appeal and appearance of the countryside. Many also complain that the turbines are noisy. Noise was a problem with early turbine designs, but this has

Wind turbines are responsible for a number of bird deaths every year.

been largely taken care of through better technology. There are also rules about how close to residential areas a company can build a wind farm.

Some environmentalists are worried about the negative impact some wind turbines have on wildlife, especially birds. Even supporters admit that turbines do kill birds. They point out, however, that the machines account for only one out of every 5,000 to 10,000 birds killed by human activity each year. Far more birds are killed by communications towers, domestic cats, and cars than by wind turbines.

In addition, every year, an estimated 97.5 million birds are killed when they fly into windows. In these cases, however, the victims are usually common birds such as sparrows and pigeons. In many cases,

Did You Know?

The Cape Wind Project

Cape Wind, an offshore wind farm planned for the coast of Massachusetts, has aroused strong feelings for and against the project. The development, if completed according to plan, would be situated in a 24-square-mile (62-square-kilometer) area of Horseshoe Shoal, off the shore of Cape Cod. The farm would include 130 turbines with an expected maximum output of 420 MW. That is enough electricity to power about three-quarters of Cape Cod and the surrounding islands of Martha's Vineyard and Nantucket. Many locals object to the project, however, which they think will destroy the natural beauty of the shoreline. (The turbines will be visible from the shore.) They also are afraid that the wind farm could harm local businesses (including fishing and tourism), pose a danger to air and sea navigation, and threaten birds, fish, and other sea life.

the birds killed by wind farms are large **raptor** species (like eagles and hawks), many of which are already at risk. Of course, the number and type of birds harmed by wind farms varies by location.

The Altamont Pass site in California, for example, seems to be responsible for hundreds of bird deaths every year. Studies have shown that as many as 300 red-tailed hawks, 116 golden eagles, 380 burrowing owls, and 333 American kestrels may be killed there every year. Experts say that Altamont is a unique case. It is located right in the middle of a raptor **migration** route, and many of its turbine rotors are spinning at just the same height at which these birds fly.

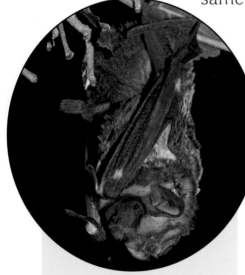

Today, Altamont serves as a warning for people who are interested in building wind farms. Environmental groups and people in the wind industry have worked together to create guidelines for safer construction. Before the construction of a wind farm is approved, environmental studies are conducted to reduce the site's impact on the area's wildlife.

Wind turbines cause thousands of bats—such as hoary bats like this one—to die each year.

Still, **conservationists** are very worried about the dangers that wind farms might pose to bats. For some time, researchers were baffled by dead bats found near wind farms. Many animals showed no outward signs of injury. They were not flying into the turbines. What, then, was killing them? Further studies showed that the bats were being killed by the rapid drop in air pressure that occurs near a turbine's blades. This was causing their lungs to bleed. According to a U.S. government report, dead bats have been found at nearly every wind power facility in North America where studies have been conducted. The researchers estimate that these sites cause thousands of bat deaths every year.

There are also other environmental concerns associated with the construction of wind farms. Large turbines require a big foundation that can be up to 165 feet (50 meters) deep. Sometimes, dynamite is used to blast holes in rocky land. Even when holes are dug using other methods, they still harm the land. Construction can disrupt local wildlife and destroy plants.

Energy In, Energy Out

Building a wind farm, or even just one turbine, requires energy. A typical turbine, however, makes up for the power used to build it after operating for about six months. After six months, whatever **pollutants** were produced in the creation of the turbine are offset by all of the pollutants the wind-powered energy keeps out of the atmosphere. A wind turbine will produce about 30 times more energy over its lifetime than was used in its construction.

It is necessary to dig a large foundation when a big turbine is built.

CHAPTER 5

What Is the Future of Wind Energy?

Although there are drawbacks associated with wind power, there are many benefits to increasing its use. Wind power seems likely to be part of the future— and not just in the United States.

The United States is currently the number one wind energy producer in the world, but many European countries have long focused on this technology. Germany, which used to be the global leader in wind energy production, generates almost 7 percent of its energy from the wind. Denmark uses wind power to meet 20 percent of its energy needs.

Fast growing nations such as China and India have also increased the number of wind turbines in their countries. In fact, in 2008, China's total capacity for wind energy production doubled for the fourth year in a row. In 2009, China was building six huge new wind power projects. Each one would be able to generate more electricity than 16 large coal-fired electrical plants. Although China still relies very heavily on traditional fossil fuels for its electricity, it is important that China begin to use more renewable power. Global energy needs are expected to increase by 44 percent by 2030, and 73 percent of this growth will occur in developing nations such as India and China. There are more than 1.3 trillion people living in China. If all of them rely on fossil fuels to meet their energy needs in the future, the effects could be **catastrophic**.

Getting Better All the Time

Engineers are constantly searching for ways to improve the construction of wind turbines, as well as how—and where—they work. Some engineers are working on double-bladed turbines that are able to "catch" more wind than traditional designs. They are also working on flying electric generators (FEGs). These turbines are tethered (attached) to the ground and flown at high altitudes of about 15,000 feet (4,570 meters). There, they can catch the strongest, steadiest winds. They would generate electric currents that would be transmitted by the **tethers** to the ground, where the electricity could join the main power grid.

Engineers at Purdue University in Indiana and Sandia National Laboratories (with locations in California and New Mexico) are working on ways to make turbines "smarter." The

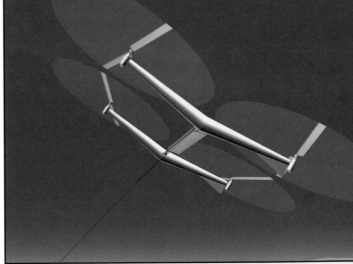

Flying electric generators are being developed. Attached to the ground, they would fly at high altitudes to catch the strongest winds.

Did You Know?

Cleaning Up Europe

In 2008, the European Union increased its wind capacity to 142 tWh, which accounts for about 4.2 percent of the continent's total demand for electricity. This increase is responsible for preventing the emission of 119 million tons (108 million metric tons) of carbon dioxide a year. That is equal to taking more than 50 million cars off the road.

Wind turbines are going to be installed on the tallest building in the United States, the Willis Tower (formerly called the Sears Tower) in Chicago, Illinois.

Did You Know?

Meeting a Developing Need

The United Nations has been creating wind maps as part of a project called the Solar and Wind Energy Resource Assessment (SWERA). SWERA maps and information provide estimates of how much wind energy is available at different sites around the world, including developing nations. So far, promising results have been found for renewable energy potential in South and Central America, Africa, and Asia.

researchers have developed a system that uses sensors and computer programs that can accurately monitor the wind. This will improve the efficiency of the turbine and prevent possible damage from winds that are too strong. The sensors are embedded right into the turbine blade.

Meanwhile, a team of engineers at the University of Wisconsin-Milwaukee has figured out a way to store the kinetic energy generated by wind turbines. The researchers

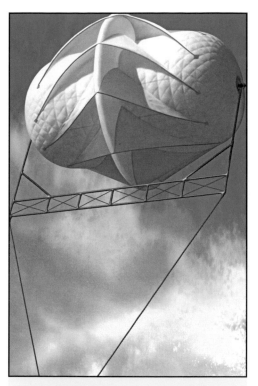

Someday, wind turbines like this may float high in the sky. Such a device would rotate around a horizontal axis when the wind blows, generating electrical energy.

In Their Own Words

"Wind energy is playing an increasing role in providing electrical power. The United States is now the largest harvester of wind energy in the world. The question is, what can be done to wind turbines to make them more efficient, more cost effective and more reliable?"

Douglas Adams, professor of mechanical engineering and director of Purdue University's Center for Systems Integrity

have created a braking control procedure that adjusts the rotor speed to take advantage of high-speed winds. Ordinarily, to prevent damage, a rotor shuts down when wind is blowing too fast. With the new system, though, the rotor is allowed to spin faster. Then, the rotor stores the excess energy as kinetic energy. Once the wind power drops, the energy is released. The team believes this **innovation** will help solve the problem of generating power when it is not windy. They also think that their new method will make turbines more efficient, so fewer will be needed at each site.

MARIA SKYLLAS-KAZACOS

Maria Skyllas-Kazacos, a chemical engineer, was born in Greece in 1951. She moved to Australia with her family when she was just two years old. She graduated from the University of New South Wales in Australia in 1974 and got a **doctoral degree** from the school four years later. After working for different companies, she became a professor at the university. In the 1980s, she led the team that invented the vanadium redox battery (VRB). "When I start off on a project I want to see its purpose," she said in an interview with the Australian Academy of Science in 2000. "I need to see that it could be important for something in the future. I also like to see a possible benefit to society." Dr. Skyllas-Kazacos has been awarded many honors for her work.

Dr. Maria Skyllas-Kazacos and the vanadium redox battery.

Yet another promising technology can be seen at a wind farm on King Island, one of the islands that make up the state of Tasmania, Australia. There, a special type of battery called a vanadium redox battery (VRB) is used to store excess electricity made from wind energy. With traditional batteries, energy is stored in a chemical form inside the battery. With the VRB, excess energy is stored in a special chemical fluid, too. When these chemicals are "filled" with energy, they are pumped out of the battery and into storage tanks. Then, more chemicals in the battery can be charged with energy. The flow is simply reversed to regenerate the energy.

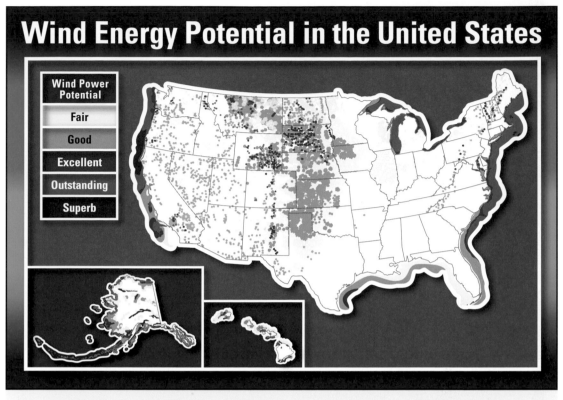

Wind Energy Potential in the United States

Wind Power Potential

- Fair
- Good
- Excellent
- Outstanding
- Superb

Many parts of the United States are windy enough to use wind power to generate energy.

In Their Own Words

"The nation that leads the world in creating new sources of clean energy will be the nation that leads the twenty-first century global economy. America must be that nation."

U.S. President Barack Obama

Whether it's in 10 years, 20 years, 30 years, or more, the day is coming when the world cannot rely as strongly as it currently does on fossil fuels to provide energy. Although no single renewable energy source can erase our reliance on fossil fuels completely, wind power will play an important role in providing energy in the future.

GLOSSARY

acid rain: Rain, snow, fog, or mist that contains acid substances and damages the environment.

atmosphere: The envelope of air that surrounds the planet.

axle: A rod that passes through the center of a wheel or gear, around which the wheel or gear turns.

carbon dioxide: A gas formed when fossil fuels are burned; also written as CO_2.

catastrophic: Disastrous.

climate: The weather and overall conditions in a place as measured over a long period of time.

conservationist: Someone who is concerned about protecting natural resources, such as wildlife and forests.

corrosive: Slowly wearing away and destroying, by the process of corrosion.

decompose: To decay or rot.

doctoral degree: The highest degree, or title, awarded by a university.

embargo: A government order restricting or prohibiting trade and other types of commerce with a specific country.

emission: A substance that is released into the air.

environment: The land, water, and air in a particular area.

fossil fuel: A fuel, such as coal, natural gas, or oil, that was formed underground over millions of years from the remains of prehistoric plants and animals. Such fuels are not renewable.

generator: A machine that is used to convert energy, such as that provided by burning fuel or by wind or water, into electricity.

glacier: A large body of ice that moves slowly across land.

global warming: The gradual warming of Earth's atmosphere and surface, caused by the buildup of carbon dioxide and other greenhouse gases that trap heat.

greenhouse gases: Gases that trap heat from the Sun within the atmosphere; carbon dioxide is one of the most common.

grid: The general electric power system.

horizontal: Running side to side, parallel to the ground.

innovation: A new invention or idea.

kinetic: Relating to motion.

lease: To agree to rent property to someone else.

manually: Operated or done by hand.

megawatt: A million watts.

migration: The movement from one area to another.

nacelle: The part of a wind turbine where the kinetic energy of the wind is turned into electricity.

nonrenewable: A resource that cannot be replaced naturally once it has been used.

panemone: A design used in early windmills.

photosynthesis: The process by which plants use energy from the Sun to turn water and carbon dioxide into food; they then give off oxygen.

pollutant: A substance that pollutes, or contaminates, something.

power plant: A place for the production of electric power, also sometimes called a "power station."

raptor: A bird of prey.

renewable: A resource, such as a source of energy, that never gets used up. Energy sources such as sunlight and wind are renewable; sources such as coal, natural gas, and oil are nonrenewable.

smog: A mixture of fog and smoke that hangs in the air over certain cities.

solar: Relating to the Sun.

sustainable: Something that can keep being used again and again without running out.

tether: A rope or chain attaching something to something else.

turbine: A machine that produces a turning action, which can be used to make electricity. The turning action may be caused by steam, wind, or some other energy source.

vertical: Running straight up and down at a right angle to the ground.

watt: A common unit of measurement for the rate at which electric energy is used.

Read these books:

Armentrout, David, and Patricia Armentrout. *Wind Energy*. Vero Beach, Florida: Rourke Publishing, 2009.

Fridell, Ron. *Earth-Friendly Energy*. Minneapolis: Lerner, 2009.

Morris, Neil. *Wind Power*. New York: Franklin Watts, 2009.

Pipe, Jim. *Wind Power—Is it Reliable Enough?* New York: Franklin Watts, 2009.

Povey, Karen D. *Energy Alternatives*. San Diego: Lucent, 2007.

Spilsbury, Richard, and Louise Spilsbury. *Wind Power*. London: Hodder Wayland, 2009.

Look up these Web sites:

Energy Kids Page
http://tonto.eia.doe.gov/kids

How Wind Power Works
http://www.howstuffworks.com/wind-power.htm

Wind with Miller: A Crash Course in Wind Energy
http://windwithmiller.windpower.org/en/kids/index.htm

Key Internet search terms:

turbine, wind, wind farm, wind power, windmill

INDEX

The abbreviation *ill.* stands for illustration, and *ills.* stands for illustrations. Page references to illustrations and maps are in *italic* type.

Acid rain 10, 11
Advantages of wind energy 24–31
Africa 40; *ill. 5*
Air pollution 9, 10, 11; *ill. 25*
Altamont Pass (California) 20, 36; *ill. 17*
Animals and plants 9, 11, 34, 35, 36, 37; *ills. 27, 34*
Atmosphere 10, 11, 14, 37
Availability of wind power 31
Axle 17, 18
Bats (animals) 36–37; *ill. 36*
Birds 35, 36; *ill. 34*
Blades (mechanical) 6, 7, 15, 17; *ill. 22*
 wind speed, effect of 16
Brakes 16
Cape Wind project 22, 23, 35
Carbon dioxide 11, 12, 17, 24, 39
Careers and employment 28, 29; *ill. 30*
China 6, 38
Climate change 12, 14

Coal 4, 9, 10, 11, 24, 34; *ills. 13, 25*
Construction of wind turbines 14–18, 37; *ill. 37*
Corrosion 33
Costs of wind power 29, 30, 33–34
Death and disease 9, 10
Demand for electricity 12, 14, 38, 39
Denmark 33, 38; *ill. 33*
Department of Energy (DOE), U.S. 13, 24, 29, 30
Design of windmills 5, 6, 7
Developers, role of 22, 27, 28, 32
Developing nations 38, 40
Drawbacks of wind power 32–37
Earth (planet) 9, 11, 12, 14
Economic benefits 27–29
Efficiency 16, 17, 37
Emissions 10, 17, 24
Environmental problems 9–12, 24, 34–37
Europe 5, 6, 22, 23, 34, 38, 39

Farmers, benefits to 27, 28
Floating wind turbines *ill. 41*
Flying electric generators 39; *ill. 39*
Formation of wind 4, 14, 20; *ill. 15*
Fossil fuels 4, 7, 9, 11, 24, 25, 38, 43
 environment, effect on 9–12
Future of wind power 38–43
Gas *see* Oil and gas
Generation of electricity 7, 8, 14, 17, 18; *ill. 31*
Germany 10, 38
Global warming 12, 24
Greenhouse gases 11, 12
Grid 8, 18, 20, 39
Grinding mills 5
Horizontal axis design 15, 17; *ill. 16*
Kinetic energy 4, 17, 40, 41
King Island (Australia) 42
Land, lease of 27, 28
Livestock 28; *ill. 27*
London (England) 10

London Array project 23, 33

Measurements of electricity 18
Micro wind turbines 18
Middle East 4, 6, 25

Nacelles 14, 17; *ill. 22*
Nitrogen oxides 10, 11
Nonrenewable energy sources *see* Fossil fuels

Offshore wind farms 21–23, 33, 35; *ill. 33*
Oil and gas 4. 9, 10, 24, 25, 26; *ill. 13*
Organization of Petroleum Exporting Countries (OPEC) 25, 26

Panemone windmills 5; *ill. 5*
Persia 6
Post mills 6
Power plants 7, 8, 11, 14, 32, 34; *ill. 25*
Putnam, Palmer 19

Raptor migration 36

Renewable energy 7, 12, 24, 40, 43; *ill. 13*
Research and experimentation 39–42
Residential uses of wind power 17, 18
Rotors 15, 36, 41

Sailboats 4; *ill. 5*
Skyllas-Kazacos, Maria 42; *ill. 42*
Smog 9
Solar and Wind Energy Resource Assessment (SWERA) 40
Solar energy 11; *ill. 13*
Soot 9, 10
Sources of energy *ill.13*
Speeds of wind 8, 16, 18
Steam 7, 14
Storage of wind power 40–41, 42
Sulfur dioxide 10, 11

Temperature 11, 12
Terrain, effect of 20, 21
Tornado 8; *ill. 8*
Tower mills 6; *ill. 7*

Transmission of electricity 8, 20, 32
Turbines 7, 8, 14–19; *ills. 16, 22*
cost of 33
improvements to 39, 40
offshore 22–23; *ill. 33*
placement of 20, 21; *ill. 40*
wildlife, impact on 35, 36

United States 9, 11, 13, 24, 38; *map 43*
energy crisis 25, 26, 27
Uses of energy 4, 12, 18
Utility companies 18, 19, 20

Vanadium redox battery 42; *ill. 42*
Vertical axis design 15; *ill. 21*

Watts 18
Wind farms 20–23, 33, 34; *ill. 17*
construction of 37
Windmills, history of 4–7

About the Author

Stephanie Fitzgerald has been writing nonfiction for children for more than 10 years, and she is the author of more than 20 books. Her specialties include history, wildlife, and popular culture. She lives in Stamford, Connecticut, with her husband, Brian, and their daughter, Molly.

DISCARDED